There once was a curious little girl
who loved to sing and dance,
pretend and watch life
unfurl.

She was the eldest of three.
loved her little brothers deeply...
you see.

Their mom and dad provided love while protecting them from harm in their quaint little home filled with promise and charm.

Their parents worked hard, providing, nurturing, and caring.
This family was uniquely woven through grace, love, and sharing.

Always
a hot meal,
doors revolving like a turning wheel,
laughter,
tears,
hugs and smiles passed around to heal.

In the safety of this home,
the little girl could imagine,
dream and explore...

She loved to read, sing and become
characters she came to adore.

When she fell and scraped her knees outside
her daddy would often say,
"No pain, no gain. Shake it off, my child."
while chuckling with pride.

If her feelings were hurt by things said or done
Mommy would say,
"you'll be alright... don't cry little one."

Inside her home, she was embraced with love.

Each night on bended knee, mommy would tuck her in with a prayer to our Lord above.

"Let the words of my mouth
and meditations of my heart
be acceptable in Thy sight...
Sleep well my rose and have sweet dreams tonight."

Outside
the world was cold and rough
for little girls like her.

You see
Each day she faced cruel words,
sneering looks,
and gestures
all because
her eyes were a blur.

Four eyes!
They'd yell across the schoolyard
even in class, she'd hear
"look at those glasses!!!"

"They're so thick!
You must be able to look into
next year!"

The words would pierce her heart
like daggers of venom, they'd sting.

She tried to ignore, shrink back,
and avoid her offenders each day,
new words they'd bring.

"Let me see your glasses!
I wanna put them on my eyes."

"maybe if I wear them
they'll make me smarter...
Four Eyes!"

They'd take her glasses, put them on
while stumbling around the school.
She'd stand there frozen in place
awaiting their return holding back tears
from the cruel ...

Cruel,

and thoughtless words
playing over and over again in her mind.

"Whew, these glasses are so thick
you must be able to see through walls!!!"
"Girl... you must be BLIND!"

You see that's just it!!!
She wanted to yell.
She couldn't respond,
her voice wouldn't tell.

        Her glasses were both a blessing and a curse.

      "You tell them you need them to see."
                    her mommy would say
          digging for a stick of gum in her purse

"I'll never forget the first day you wore them"
While reminiscing mommy said,
"You were a year old
just a baby with the tiniest little face.
The doctor made them especially for you
from doll frames just so they'd stay in place."

"Look at the birds, the flowers, the trees"
"You shouted with excitement when we came home."

"You felt free to explore and walk about without my hand, you could roam."

"I felt guilty for waiting so long ... remembering your auntie's words like words of a song."

"Take that baby to the doctor! Something's wrong with her eyes."
"she sits too close to the TV!"

"There's nothing wrong with my baby girl! She's just filled with curiosity."

As the little girl grew with wonder and splendor,
each day was an opportunity to flourish, all the more.

With each passing day,
she heightened rapidly in stature.
Her legs deeply rooted
connected to the earth
were long by nature.

She loved being outdoors,
playing with her brothers,
and tried her hand at every sport.

Track and field,
softball,
basketball,
tennis,
volleyball,
to name a few...

Even drill team,
cheerleading,
the world was a game.

A symphony in her mind
but outward coordination was not her fame.

"Your girl has great height.
Sign her up for basketball.
We'll get her coordinated"
one coach said to her dad.

"Alright OK! "Just say when and she's there! "
"My daughter can do anything!"
"She's got the legs for it,
we'll just have to get her out of her head!"

Each practice was tough...
The ball just went all around.

"We gotta get her head in the game,"
the coach said.
"That height can't go to waste"
"She's fast and agile,
just hasn't made a shot yet!"

"Don't give up on her!"
dad said.
"My girl's talent bound!"

This girl was excited and ready for her first game, fresh new uniform, perfectly laced shoes, and motivation to try something new.

Before practice one day she was the first pick on a spontaneous volleyball game in the park.

Her team won every volley!

She cleared to hit one over the net but didn't see in her peripheral someone coming with their hands toward hers, knocked off her glasses and back went her hand with the ball.

A long wait in the ER. Later, multiple fractures and no sports for six weeks at all.

Over the phone, she could hear her dad say,

"How did she break her finger playing volleyball during basketball season?"

"She'll be on the bench for her first game tomorrow!"

In school, she sat as close to the board as possible...
Inquisitive by nature, she didn't want to miss a beat.

Often glued to the words of her teachers.
Their words played like records in her memory stored...

She loved to learn and found thrill in knowing her mind was like a sponge quickly absorbing,

She'd write and read,
read and write
and do it again with great delight.

Inside the classroom, she soared like an eagle with wings aglow, wanting answers, questioning, wondering about history, science

just to know...

But... outside on the yard, in the halls especially when adults weren't around, her name may as well have been mud.

"Hey, Four Eyes...
tell me my future, I know you can see it well!"
"With glasses like that you have to see into tomorrow!!!"
"Do they make your brain swell?!!!"

Even in the store,
Sometimes with Mommy around, grownups would say...

"Wow!!! Man, those are the biggest glasses I've ever seen!"
"They must be heavy ...not that I'm trying to be mean"

"They're not heavy they were especially made with love!"
Mommy would say.

The girl would want to disappear or hide,
she didn't like to be made a spectacle of...

Time and time again it would happen...

They would always bring it up ...

Even if she was dressed in her fanciest get-up...

Even at a nice restaurant once she caught people pointing and jesting.

They held Coca-Cola bottles up to their eyes and said...
"Guess who I am?!"

Then a whole table went to laughing.

They looked around and saw tears streaming down the girl's eyes.
"We didn't mean anything by it... just having fun!"
"Don't take it so personal we're just messing around!"

Middle school came around and the girl
was excited to meet new friends,
take the school bus,
and have a locker...

just to be on her own.

Didn't take long for them to find her,
even in a new school,
they would single her out without fail.

In order to stay out of the spotlight the girl sat quietly on the bus,
reading,
thinking,
or even noticing stark patterns in the clouds
like puffs of lovely packs of birds, schools of fish,
maybe even a whale.

Her thoughts were interrupted by shoves or backpacks dumped in her seat.

"Scoot over Four eyes. I need to sit down!"

Some were not even polite enough
to utter good morning or properly greet.

As the bus filled with young riders, some were anxiously ready to get to school

Talks of campus celebrations,
class competitions,
basketball games and even science projects permeated the air.

As soon as the driver stopped...
they'd rush off the bus almost in stampede fashion ready to conquer.

The girl would make haste to her locker bay, in a rush to make it before he could get there first.

For weeks now a boy would
lurk
in her locker bay and find different ways to give her a morning adventure.

Sometimes, he'd quietly wait for her to twist and turn her final combination number in and then he'd swoop in and slam the locker shut.

This could go on for what seemed like forever for the girl sometimes until just before the first bell.

Once he was gone she quickly grabbed her books and used her feet to dash down to her morning class.

When the boy was filled with even more mischief
he'd wait for her to be alone in her locker bay
and come behind her and snatch her glasses off of her face.

He'd wear them and stumble around the halls
"Look at me! Guess who I am?"
He'd giggle and laugh shrieking and clowning to get a laugh from anyone noticing in that space,
Inside she'd tell herself,
"Don't cry... don't let him see your embarrassment or shame"

Sometimes her tears would betray her and...

his words would echo like a distant drum as he tossed her glasses back and forth She felt helpless, almost numb

"Lighten up Four Eyes!"

Inside her head she'd yell, scream maybe even shout
that's not
my name!!!"

School days got longer and longer.

Middle school brought on awkward moments
accented by the fact that some challenges were a little exaggerated by those glasses.

Challenges like running the mile for a timed test
when the girl was determined to get under 8 minutes.

With sweat dripping down her face and...
while holding those lenses in place.

So, that she would be able to see the lanes she did it
and crossed the finish line with a big smile.

The coach clocked her at 7 minutes 59 seconds.

"Why don't you put straps on those glasses so you don't have to hold them?"
She just smiled and nodded, thinking to herself,
"Do you think I need anything else with these lenses drawing more attention?!!!"
"Straps are great for 60-year-olds
not an 11 year old trying to go unnoticed instead..."

Bus rides got even longer
Paper tossed in her seat...

Signs were placed in reserved spaces. (written by her fan club)

Anyone can sit here but her ... (pointing toward the girl)

"Four Eyes!"

Mr. Driver, "I think she should have to pay more to ride this bus her glasses are so big she needs two seats it's unfair to the rest of us!"

One day she was summoned to the office a place she had only been to a few times before...

"Sit down we want to talk about what's been happening to you.."
Before she sat she could hear her parents' voices on speakerphone talking to the assistant principal with concern in their voices.

She looked up with deeply saddened eyes. Tears began to flow. Her parents were saying,

"Why didn't you tell us he was treating you this way?
We would have stopped it... It's not acceptable!"
"He will be punished we want you to know!"

She noticed the boy already sitting in the office. Ashamed to look up and avoiding a chance for their eyes to meet.

"I didn't want anyone to get in trouble just wanted to be left alone. Who told you anything was happening?"

"It stops today,"
they all agreed.

"He must learn a lesson."

While mornings in the locker bay were much more pleasant, the kids on the bus turned their antics way up!

Just a few days before Christmas break the girl was determined to take matters into her own hands.

She'd had enough but had an idea about a way to take a stand.

"Mommy please take me shopping!"

"I want to make Christmas gift bags,"
she explained in the car ride over her plan to end this once and for all.

Her mom was all in with the girl's heart in mind.

"I need a gift for every rider!"
said the girl.

"Something to let them know the importance of being kind."

Her mom helped her select gifts just right for each schoolmate
They wrapped each gift with a special touch and flair.

The next morning, she was dressed and ready with anticipation.
She stepped onto the bus beaming, dazzling...

Greeting each rider with a bright smile. As they received her gifts...
Many were shocked,
rendered speechless,
even questioning her motivation.

Once all gifts were passed out
mutterings
of conversations began.

"I can't believe she bought us all gifts...
We've been so cruel to her.
I don't even understand!"
Said a girl in one breath.

As the school day went on the girl went through each class with such an overwhelming sense of peace.

She found people waving to her throughout the day, making small talk

Not treating her like the girl with the
Four Eye disease!!!

Back on the bus
the last day of school before winter break...

They were pumped with sugary treats...

Some talked over their Christmas plans, and family vacations and swapped ideas for their Christmas wish list.

When the girl walked on and looked for a seat a hush came over the riders almost at once.

"There's a seat over here,"
one rider said.

"She's sitting next to me,"
one boldly said.

"I need to make an announcement!"
she said with authority.

(She was one that always commanded an audience,
whose voice was often heard above the rest.)

"I'm sorry for all the mean things I've said to you,"
looking at the girl with great conviction in her eyes.

Another rider expressed herself with a teary plea.
"Please forgive me!" "I know better!" "My mother taught me to stand up for people who are picked on or bullied!"

One after another they voluntarily tried to make things right.

It was a sweet moment ...

They all were talking and sharing about times they were treated poorly by someone

or

had someone call them names out of spit.e

"So what made you give us all gifts? We truly don't deserve any of these nice things!"

"I was thinking of a way to share kindness packaged in small gifts to take away the sting"

"Every day I entered this bus just wanting, hoping to be left alone....!"

"My glasses have always been a magnet for attention sparking questioning looks about the unknown"

"Why are your glasses so thick? How long have you had to wear them?"

This time the questions were genuine not taunts poking away for shame.

"I was born legally blind," she said.

They listened intently as if they really wanted to understand.

"Why can't they make smaller glasses for you?"

"Maybe one day someone will…. Until then I'll wait until I'm old enough to wear contact. lenses."

More and more…

The conversation lightened….

As the story ends the teacher begins closing the book slowly...

"Wait!"

A student objects.

"I really want to know what happens to the girl?!"

"Well," said the teacher.

"She grew up to share her story with children through her life's work..."

"She dedicates time to give a voice to students treated like her."

"That little, girl AKA: Four Eyes has a name You see... You could be seeing her when you see me..."

Author's Page

Yvette Martin endured bullying as a school aged child. She would write as an outlet during these formative years. This fueled a life long career for being a champion for young learners. Eventually, she charted a path that focused on the benefits of providing access to education for all. It has allowed her to be an advocate for students who are vulnerable to bullying.

Her voice is giving life to untold stories...

Dedication

This story is dedicated to...

The unmatched love of my life, my amazing husband Dr. Antwon Martin.

My brilliant, beautiful and loving daughters Hannah Rose Martin and Faith Abigail Martin.

My parents who planted seeds of creativity that sparked the writers pen.

Made in the USA
Columbia, SC
21 June 2024

37323994R00020